Reiki: A Practical Guide
Bill Waites and Master Naharo

Like a radio that can be switched on to pick up invisible signals, our hands are instruments waiting to be instructed on how to channel invisible, yet very powerful energies. When gathered, this energy can be used to heal the body, mind and spirit.

This is the basis of the ancient art of Reiki, which originated in the East, and which continues to be practiced today by masters worldwide. While Reiki may utilize the hands, it need not use touch as a transmitter. The reader will be taken through the steps of determining the aura, or energy field around the body, and learn how to apply Reiki to the physical body as well as to our spiritual nature.

This book was created for use with the human spirit, but it doesn't stop there. You have the power to channel energy for your household pets and plants.

Bill Waites is a lawyer and an economist. Waites gave up a flourishing legal practice and business to study Reiki at its source in India, China and Japan, in order to learn Reiki at its source. This book is a reflection of his spiritual journey. **Master Naharo** is a 73-year-old Indian master from Poona. He is a well-known guru in the East. Master Naharo was Bill Waites' first teacher.

ASTROLOG - THE HEALING SERIES

Holistic Healing
Rachel Lewin

Feng Shui
Richard Taylor and Wang Tann

Reiki
Bill Waites and Master Naharo

Reiki

A Practical Guide

Bill Waites and Master Naharo

Astrolog Publishing House

Astrolog Publishing House
P.O.Box 1123, Hod Hasharon 45111, Israel
TEL/FAX. 972-9-7412044
E-Mail: info@astrolog.co.il
Astrolog Web Site: www.astrolog.co.il

ISBN 965-494-046-9

Published by Astrolog Publishing House 1998

Distribution:
U.S.A & CANADA by APG - associated publishers group
U.K & EUROPE by DEEP BOOKS
EAST ASIA by CKK Ltd

Printed in Israel
10 9 8 7 6 5 4 3 2 1

Introduction

A few years ago, on a business trip to London, I left my hotel at dawn, as is my habit, to go for a jog in the local public park. During those years, I always stayed in a hotel for businessmen near Marble Arch. As I ran, I passed the spot where the royal executioner had beheaded victims many years ago; I continued on into the broad paths of the beautifully cultivated public park. There is a certain magic about a jog on a cool morning with the mist still hovering over the expansive lawns, and the treetops almost invisible in the faint morning light.

Besides the fairly large number of joggers and cyclists, the park was dominated by dogs taking their morning walks. Their owners, sitting bundled up in thick coats on park benches, let their dogs run free, and the animals did their best to trip up the joggers and cyclists.

Since I followed the same route each day, I quickly became familiar with the park's characteristics. A small, elderly lady would sit alone each morning on an isolated bench at the edge of the lane. The woman herself did not attract my attention, but rather the large number of dogs who gathered by her bench from all over the park. Her bench was at the end of my route, and every morning I would stand at a short distance from her and her dogs doing my stretching and relaxation exercises.

A strange ritual was performed daily by the woman and the dogs that surrounded her. She sat erect on the bench, and every now and then, one of the dogs would approach her and stand within arm's reach. The woman would stretch out her hand, place her palm between the dog's eyes, and remain that way for about a minute. When she removed her hand, each of the dogs would make a licking movement, nod its head as if thanking her, and then move away. Although there were at least half a dozen dogs around the bench, only one would approach her at a time, and until it had moved away, none of the other dogs would approach the woman.

It was a mysterious ritual, and it seemed to me that certain rules had been determined by the woman and the dogs - similar, for example, to those in the queue at a doctor's clinic.

After a few days, I could no longer contain my curiosity and approached the woman. Close up, I could discern that she was about 60 years old and of Asian descent. Although the morning visitors to the park generally greeted each other with a "good morning" or a polite nod of the head, she seemed surprised by my greeting.

This was the first time I had heard about Reiki, and although this pleasant woman took the time to explain that she was performing Reiki on the dogs, and that they came to her to be cured of disease or pain, I did not really understand her meaning. However, after listening to her explain her actions, I understood why the image of a doctor's clinic had entered my mind: The dogs actually looked like visitors to an eccentric healer with special powers.

Passing a bookshop, I purchased three books with the word "Reiki" in their title and read them eagerly during my flight from London to Los Angeles.

This was my first step toward becoming a "Reiki Master". (Two years later, I decided to travel to India and Japan to study Reiki.) It was also the first step in the long journey which brought me to write this book, which I dedicated to that mysterious woman – whose name I will never know – sitting in the park and wordlessly treating the local dogs.

Reiki is a Japanese term meaning "energetic spirit." It is composed of two words. The second word, *Ki*, is known in other cultures as *Chi* (China), *Prana* (India),

Shakti (in Yoga), vitality (in the West) or *Ru'ach Chayim* (Judaism). In other words, this term is present in all cultures, and relates to the superior, all-encompassing cosmic energy from which all other minor energies in the universe draw their power.

Getting back to the first word, *Rei* is a general term for spirit or unseen spiritual quality, which serves as a channel or container for the *Ki*.

Many terms in different cultures speak of similar qualities. Whether called "Godly Spirit" or "Life Energy," the "Etheric Body" or "Cosmic Energy," the meaning is the same: There is an inexhaustible source of energy which may, if we know how to tap it, be conveyed through some sort of channel, revitalizing a living body (not necessarily the human body) and improving its quality of life both physically and spiritually.

In the West, the word *Reiki* is usually used, since the use of Reiki facilitates healing with this spiritual energy through a "channel". (The process itself is known as "channeling".)

Put simply, Reiki is an ancient known healing technique, in which healing is performed by the touch of a hand, in the same manner that a mother covers her child's injury with her hand, or a holy man or Shaman touches a sick person. However, Reiki affords us additional tools relating to touch, mainly allowing us to direct the flow of energy from a limitless source to the patient, in a meditative, spiritual manner, via the "tool" - in other words, the Reiki Master.

That is to say, Reiki teaches us how to be a channel for this limitless, ever-flowing energy, while enabling each individual to become an energy channel and draw the benefits of the *Ki* to himself and his patients.

It is easy to learn Reiki at a two-day course which, providing it is taught by a certified teacher, is useful and effective. This is the easy way. The harder way is not only to learn Reiki, but to *understand* it, and this route demands that the student-reader delve deeply into the text in an attempt to comprehend the essence which lies beneath the Reiki phenomenon.

I have chosen to present Reiki through a series of personal stories, some of which I experienced myself, and some of which I heard from patients and other Reiki teachers. I am grateful to all those whose stories helped pave the way.

Above all, I am thankful to the great Master, a Reiki teacher and guide, who showed me the way and revealed the light that is in Reiki to me: My teacher, Master Naharo.

What happened the very first time?

When I arrived in Poona, I had never met or even heard of Master Naharo, my esteemed teacher. Indeed, I had gone there seeking to learn the arts of Eastern meditation, and while I had a general understanding of what Reiki was, it was no more than that.

At the time, I was suffering from extreme lower back pain and had been treated by various doctors – some of whom were "alternative" practitioners – who helped relieve my pain.

One treated me for a herniated disk, another addressed the muscular spasm, another assessed my nutrition, while another stuck fine needles all over my body. It all helped ... but only temporarily!

I journeyed to Poona in an old bus carrying at least two hundred passengers – three or four to each seat, others clinging on to every possible surface, including the roof and sides of the bus – cursing the pain in my back all the way.

Each pothole, each bend, caused me to scream in agony. When the bus finally reached its destination, I alighted, my body distorted into the shape of a question mark, and barely capable of dragging my backpack along behind me.

"May Heaven bless you," said a soft voice beside me.

My hand went into my pocket and I turned around, ready to place a rupee in the speaker's palm.... however, instead of finding a smiling beggar – in India, mainly in Poona and such places, even beggars smile and radiate light and gentleness – I saw Anka, as I later discovered she was called.

Anka was a Dutchwoman, probably about 50 years old but with the smile and demeanor of a 20-year-old girl. Nothing about her was what you might call beautiful or special, but all around her was a light, a sort of halo, so that anyone who saw her felt an immediate sense of warmth.

"I see that your back is bothering you," she said gently. "Are you on your way to the Master?"

"No, I haven't got plans to see anyone in particular," I answered, embarrassed. "I've just arrived."

"Come with me," she said.

These few words changed my life. She lifted my backpack and walked slowly away down the dusty road, without looking back. I hurried after her as best I could.

Twenty painful minutes later, a white stone building came into view, modest but well kept, surrounded by a brown stone wall. Beside the wall, near the large gate, were several dozen people, mostly locals, sitting in silence. Each one seemed rapt in his own world.

"Wait here," Anka said.

She placed my backpack on a stone bench inside the gate. I could barely sit down. The line of waiting people continued into the inner courtyard; a long line moving suitably slowly, with someone entering the side entrance to the building now and again. Others came out of the door passed through the gate before disappearing around the bend.

I waited there for half an hour – time, in the Western sense, has no meaning in India – until Anka returned. She carried a clay jug full of cool water and a wide-brimmed mug, which she placed beside me before vanishing once again.

I lost all track of time. The line grew shorter, until at one point, a tall, slim, Indian man came out, muttered a few words, and the remaining people rose and left silently. Anka entered the courtyard immediately behind him.

"Follow me," she said.

Inside the house it was cool and pleasant. We passed through a large hall and into a square room filled with light. In the center of the room was a long, high wooden table. Standing next to the table was an Indian man of about 50 (Master Naharo always looks younger than his age; he was in fact about 70 at the time), folding a white cotton sheet.

"Remove your sandals," Anka told me.

I obeyed, and walked to the center of the room, wondering what awaited me there. The Indian man then addressed me in fluent English, introduced himself as Naharo and welcomed me to his country. He asked several questions concerning my journey to Poona, and in just a few minutes I had the feeling he had known me for years. Suddenly, he reached out his hand and laid it on my right shoulder.

Indian people do not generally touch one another. Every Indian respects his fellow's personal body space, and physical contact between them is quite rare. I was astounded at first, but then I experienced a strange sensation: A wave of heat spread down my body, washing over me like a wave of warm water. As the heat flooded through me, the back pain that had caused me such suffering disappeared.

I do not recall that he said anything to me. All I remember is lying face down on a table covered with a sheet, with the man standing beside me passing the palms of his hands along my back. Anka joined in and they both passed their palms along my back and legs.

That day, I stayed in the spacious home of Master Naharo: one week later, I had resolved to become his devoted student – and not simply because my terrible back pain had vanished. During that week, on a daily basis, I observed the people coming to see the Master – people who came to him filled with mental and physical pain, and who left smiling, the pain under control, their spirits strengthened. It seemed that Master Naharo planted a kernel of light in each person.

I saw his disciples, both those who lived in his house and those who lived in Poona, arriving at his house each morning. There were Indians, Englishmen, Frenchmen, Germans, Italians, Chinese, Japanese, Israelis ... it seemed that people from all over the world managed to find their way to the Master.

Despite the diversity of cultures, ages and occupations, they all had one thing in common: They were all energized and full of vitality, as if incredibly enlightened. It seemed that each person had fulfilled his utmost personal potential!

I also wanted to be like that.

Thus it was that a chance encounter with Anka brought me to the Master, who changed my life and made me into a better person, allowing me to contribute to the those around me to the best of my ability. I only pray that the important task that rests on my shoulders does not prove too much for my meager powers.

The Five Supreme Principles of Reiki

Unfortunately, human beings cannot learn a new way of life unless they are first presented with the principles, philosophy and milestones of that new approach. By nature, these principles are worded concisely, in a manner which is easy on the memory, and constitute the basis of the entire doctrine.

The study of Reiki also includes these principles, known as the "Five Principles". However, since each Grand Master of Reiki, or great teacher, has devised his own principles, there is a difference between studying with one Master and studying with another. Some teachers propound four fundamental principles while others propound seven.

Setting the number of principles at five suits the Chinese way of thinking. They believe that the number five is the most basic of all numbers, the proof being the five elements (as opposed to the four elements of Western culture). Therefore, setting the number of principles at five is compatible with Chinese culture, one which has influenced the entire East.

1

The first principle of Reiki is the principle of anger, or, more precisely, *non*-anger. Anger, whether at oneself, at others or at the whole world, creates serious blockages in one's energy. This situation can be compared to a farmer whose fields are irrigated by water channels. Anger is like the large boulders which block the flow of water in the channels. Some fields are quickly flooded and their crops rot; others remain dry and their crops die of drought!

Anger is an individual's most complex inner enemy. Far from being fleeting, it becomes an integral part of one's personality. At the beginning, you may be angry at someone for one reason or another (and generally without any reason at all). Later you *remember* that you were angry at him and your anger is fired both by the thought that it was justified, and by guilt feelings that you were angry for nothing. And so, layer after layer of anger accumulates, and the nucleus of your anger turns into a great mountain of anger blocking the flow of energy and requiring a great effort for its removal.

Reiki, as a tool which directs cosmic energy to the place *where it is required*, is an excellent device for removing anger blockages which have accumulated in the body. However, the student reading this book should not be misled: All the Reiki treatments in the world will not overcome anger if the individual does not *cease* being angry. Reiki can remove anger blockages which have accumulated over the years (and, at times, even those which are a result of past lives). But Reiki cannot remove the residue of recurrent anger which occurs daily. This has been compared to a dog chasing its tail!

Do not be angry! This is the first principle of Reiki.

2

The second principle of Reiki is the principle of worry, or more precisely, the principle of *not* worrying. If a person's anger involves processes in which the individual relates to the past or present (we do not usually get angry at something that is yet to happen), the principle of worry deals with future events.

People, especially nowadays, have many reasons to worry about what the future holds. What will happen if I am fired from my job tomorrow? What will happen if I fall ill? What will happen if my favorite basketball team loses? What will happen to the rain forests in Brazil? What will be... ? Endless worries may fill one's head, and each one bores a small hole in one's body and soul.

Returning to the example above, anger is compared to boulders blocking the flow of energy, while worry is compared to large worms that bore through the walls of the water channels, causing them to crumble and leading to a leakage of water (energy) from the channel.

As opposed to anger, which requires a focused Reiki treatment in order to remove the obstacle, worry demands that Reiki energy spread throughout the entire body. Instead of removing the block, it seals and repairs thousands of small "holes". And as opposed to what a novice might think, it is much harder to treat problems relating to worry than those rooted in anger.

An individual who has experienced Reiki will quickly learn not to be angry, but it is much more difficult to teach such a person not to worry. Moreover, those who experience Reiki treatments are usually sensitive by nature, with hearts and souls that are open to the world and to society... And these are the exact foundations upon which worry is built.

In addition, it must be remembered that worry is not always a negative phenomenon. Let us assume that you are a mother whose young son must cross the street every day on his way to school. Naturally, you are concerned about his welfare, so you warn him repeatedly about crossing only on the crosswalk, and worry daily until the moment when he enters the house safe and sound. Is it logical to suggest that you refrain from worrying? No. As a result of your concern for your child, you warn him to cross at a safe crosswalk, thereby helping him to protect himself. In other words, in this case, worry is a positive force, even though it is useful for one party (the child) while it drives the other party (the mother) out of her mind. What can a Reiki teacher do in this case? In addition to Reiki treatments, the teacher will have to find a middle ground in order to ease the mother's concern; for example, suggesting that the mother accompany her son to the crosswalk every day, or that she organize a voluntary crossing guard to man the crosswalk during those hours when children's safety is at stake.

Do not worry! This is the second principle of Reiki. Easy to say, but difficult to apply.

3

The third principle of Reiki is a positive principle – not one that instructs us *not* to be angry or *not* to worry, but one that may be expressed by the phrase, "Be grateful." A Reiki teacher that I once met claimed that if you smile at three different people throughout your day, you have fulfilled this principle. This is the essence of the principle – a smile, a good word, gratitude, thanks, forgiveness... simple things that might seem to be merely common courtesy, but which improve one's life and make one happier.

Remember that this principle is not only an external one. If you smile at everyone, always say "please" and "thank you", *but do not mean it*, you have not done anything at all for yourself (even if you have made others feel better).

The important element in this principle is inner intention, which is the only thing that benefits the individual.

My esteemed teacher defined it in the following way: " When a person is truly grateful, he radiates inner light and illuminates his surroundings. When a person is seemingly grateful but not does mean it, he is illuminated by an external light which originates outside of him but does not penetrate the aura enveloping him. Therefore, we might put it this way: Be grateful from your heart inward. This is the third principle of Reiki."

It is easy to apply this principle. It improves a person's life and the lives of those around him.

4

The fourth principle of Reiki is a general principle, simply stated: "Live a life of honor." This principle has many interpretations, although most teachers prefer to word it concisely and leave its interpretation to the individual himself.

The term *honor* means something different in every culture, and each Reiki teacher and student is fully aware of what the principle of honor means in his society. It should be remembered that honor exists amongst prisoners in jail, soldiers in the army, members of a family, teachers and pupils in schools, and so on.

Some teachers express this principle in a slightly different manner: "Earning a respectable living." In other words, support yourself and your family respectably, without harming others. This is an important principle in Buddhism, for example.

(Later on in this book, I will discuss one of the Reiki principles that many teachers have adopted. Reiki, as a treatment or as training, should not given for free, and a "stiff" fee should be charged. These teachers base their actions on the fourth principle, thereby distorting the true meaning of the words.)

5

The fifth principle of Reiki is that of honoring family, teachers and society, or, in other words, "Honor your parents, honor your teachers, honor your elders."

It seems to me that this rule should be obvious to everyone. Honoring the family protects family unity and creates a comfortable and positive environment for the individual and improves his daily life. Honoring teachers emphasizes the importance of knowledge and wisdom passed on from one generation to the next by the wise teachers of each generation. And one must remember to respect any person who has taught you something, whether he is an enlightened individual or just a simple teacher. Honoring our elders helps each of us remember that life is only a transitional stage between birth and death, and those close to the gates of death have already acquired much life experience and must therefore be respected.

These, then, are the five principles of Reiki which every teacher and student must master: *Do not be angry, do not worry, be grateful, live a life of honor, and honor your parents, teachers and elders.* This is the entire Reiki philosophy.

Reiki and Initiation

In the distant past and up to a few years ago, Reiki was simply an oral doctrine – a philosophy or method based on an oral tradition transmitted from teacher to student over the generations, as opposed to one based on writings ("sacred texts") serving as an instruction manual for the study. Therefore, a Reiki "graduate" is certified through initiation, and not through study and qualifying examinations.

Initiation is a method through which the certified Reiki instructor, master or "grand" master, works with a group of students, teaches them the principles of Reiki, equips them with the "key words" or symbols, and certifies them as Reiki healers or teachers (according to the level of the course). In short, this is the process of initiation.

In every initiation process, the most important thing

is the relationship between teacher and student. In Reiki, this connection is far more crucial, since the teacher, through the Reiki technique, leaves an imprint of something of himself upon the student. Moreover, in the process of transmitting symbols, known as the second level of Reiki – which allows for treatment from a distance – the teacher passes on certain symbols to the student. The first symbol is usually the symbol which creates the relationship between teacher and student, and is therefore common to both of them. When I received the symbols from my esteemed teacher, Master Naharo, the first symbol was the water buffalo. At the time, I did not really think about this symbol. It was just one of five symbols which I received during my initiation qualifying me as a second-level Reiki healer, and as an initiate on my way to becoming a Reiki Master and a Grand Master – a stage I had not yet reached. However, during one of my extended stays in Poona, I discovered that my teacher's fifth symbol was the water buffalo.

In the East, the water buffalo symbolizes a creature which is very beneficial to the farmer, helping him to work the land and carry loads while demanding very little in return. It symbolizes a consistent person who does not stray from the path leading to his predestined goal, whose every step affects his surroundings in a positive manner.

In this way, when the teacher's last symbol becomes the student's first, the Reiki tradition is preserved and a chain of transmission of the doctrine from generation to generation is created.

At the same time, do not forget that the iniation, with all its advantages, is riddled with dangers, the first being the situation in which a charlatan teacher certifies students. Such a situation leads to a proliferation of students graduating from Reiki training, convinced that they are on the correct path, but actually continue to spread false teaching.

Therefore, in Reiki, or other teachings based on initiation, it is of the utmost importance to choose the right teacher.

Unfortunately, there are many Reiki teachers plying their trade on every street corner; they do not teach the pure, true Reiki which aims only to be of benefit to the individual. These teachers are only interested in their financial gain. The various courses are quite expensive, as are the treatments, which do not usually have long-term benefits – and it is all at the expense of their students and patients. The humility and modesty which were typical of the great teachers have disappeared, replaced by the ostentatious advertisements of seemingly trendy teachers.

The student coming to study Reiki and receive certification, must examine his prospective teacher and his path carefully. If not, any initiation will be a waste of time. This is not so simple, however. How can we expect an inexperienced student to differentiate between a true Reiki teacher and an impostor, when even experienced, well-known teachers turn out to be charlatans who have succeeded in fooling other teachers?

I can only offer one simple way to do so: Open your heart! The student wishing to enter into initiation must open his heart and soul when he meets the teacher. If a relationship develops between them, this is the right teacher for him. If he feels the slightest distress or discomfort, it would be preferable to seek a different teacher.

Another suggestion: Learn about the topic before you begin your studies. Today, as opposed to the past, there are many books which teach the Reiki method (even though the initiation must still be received personally from the teacher).

It must be remembered and taken into account that the initiation creates a dependence between student and teacher. During one of my lecture tours, I encountered this phenomenon in the south of England. A Reiki teacher, very knowledgeable, but lacking the moral purity required for a Reiki Master, became the focal point of a large group of Reiki students. She would divide the Reiki course into many "slices": A preliminary introductory course, a beginner's Reiki course, a course based on the first principle, a course based on the second principle, etc. Thus the students only received a certificate for the second level of Reiki after having completed 17 courses. Between each pair of courses, the teacher required a break of at least two weeks, during which the students participated in "training and practice" – for a fee, of course. An average student would spend about a year with the teacher and pay about $60,000. Clearly, Reiki had became a tool for extorting money and could therefore not benefit the students. When I arrived in the area and offered a two-day, weekend first-level Reiki course for $300, the teacher offered me $10,000 in return for getting out of her "territory". Obviously, this phenomenon does not contribute to Reiki at all.

On the other hand, in Canada, I met two French Reiki teachers who gave first- and second-level Reiki courses over the weekend, at a small rural farm. The students paid a modest fee, about $150, and each brought a small gift for the weekend: a home-made cake, a casserole or a plant. When I arrived, I could immediately feel the good atmosphere. It seemed as if the place was "illuminated" and I felt a pleasant warmth at the light radiating from the students' eyes. Although the temperature was way below zero, the feeling was similar to that in the illuminated places in Poona where I had studied. From that time on, I try to return to that small farmhouse at every opportunity and join in the Reiki activities, strengthening my powers by exchanging energy with the local teachers and students. I advise all Reiki teachers to take this example to heart.

How is a Reiki treatment performed?

Reiki seems much more mysterious when spoken about than when actually seen. Although, to a certain extent, a Reiki treatment involves intimate touch between healer and patient, it is advisable that every person who intends to study Reiki observe an actual treatment before beginning his studies.

At this point, we will attempt to describe all the stages of a treatment involving touch – first-level Reiki – given by a healer to a patient.

The patient, a man of about 40 years old, enters a small room in which the healer is already waiting. She is a woman of about 50 years old, with graying hair and shining eyes, wearing a colorful cotton dress and no shoes.

He is wearing ordinary, loose-fitting clothes. The healer asks him to remove his shoes and leave them outside the room. He does so, and reenters in his stockinged feet.

Meanwhile, the healer has lit a candle under a small dish containing essential oil, spreading a pleasant aroma throughout the small room. Soft music is playing on a tape recorder sitting on the floor. There is no electric light source and the room is illuminated by daylight coming through a wide window veiled by a semi-transparent curtain. The healer receives him and briefly explains the essence of Reiki. This pleasant conversation lasts a few minutes. Next they move on to the treatment itself.

The healer asks the man to climb on to a high, narrow treatment table covered with a white sheet. The table is standing in the center of the room so that the healer has access to the patient from both sides. The man lies down on his back, as the healer instructs him to, with his legs slightly apart and his arms resting at his side. She places a small pillow under his neck and covers his body loosely with a white cotton sheet.

[The small pillow under *the nape of his neck* helps open the upper chakras. The sheet covering him is effective in three ways: First, during the Reiki treatment, a treatment filled with emotional responses, the patient may perspire, shiver with cold or feel waves of heat (and at times, all of the above, intermittently), and the sheet helps balance him physically. Second, the sheet affords the patient, who is often put in an unpleasant situation by the healer, a feeling of safety. Third, the sheet generally prevents any sort of contact that could be conceived as sexual – absolutely forbidden between healer and patient; since Reiki requires contact between the healer's hands and the patient's body, this danger exists.]

After the patient has relaxed on the table, the healer approaches a small basin and washes her hands with running water and dries them on a small white towel. Remember that the palms of the hands are the most important tool in first-level Reiki and must therefore be kept clean and in working order.

The healer approaches and stands at the head of the table, behind the patient's head. She places her palms on the patient's head, so that his eyes are covered; her fingers are near his mouth and the heel of her hand is resting on his forehead. Almost unconsciously, the healer's breathing and the breathing of the patient reach a similar rhythm. When this rhythm is achieved, the practical stage of the Reiki treatment may begin. The patient will generally feel a sense of warmth while the healer feels tingling in her palms.

The healer holds her hands still for a few minutes with her eyes partially closed. At a certain point, she begins to move her hands downwards alongside the patient's head, chin, throat and shoulders. The movements develop into small circles, the right hand moving clockwise and the left moving counter-clockwise. Every now and then, the movement ceases and the healer holds her hands over a certain spot for a few minutes. The patient trembles occasionally but the overall feeling is one of sleepiness.

At this point, the healer moves to one side of the table and continues gently touching the surface of the patient's body with circular motions, until she reaches his feet. When she does reach his feet, about half an hour will have elapsed since he entered the room.

[It is important to note that the healer herself determines the speed at which she moves her hands, according to an inner sense which develops over time and with experience. Let the hands move when they want to! But at the same time, construct a solid, precise, overall plan for Reiki treatment.]

Now, the healer supports the patient, helping him roll over on to his left side, with his legs slightly bent, as if he assuming the fetal position. The healer remains behind him and begins the treatment again, from the head (above the right ear), along the entire right side, down to the right foot. Having completed the treatment, she helps the patient roll on to his right side, moves behind his back, and performs the treatment on his left side, from head to foot. By now, about an hour will have passed.

Now the patient lies on his stomach. He appears sleepy but his body still trembles occasionally. The healer is standing on his right side and is performing Reiki from the head downwards. The main area she is treating now is the spinal cord, along its length and down both sides of it. Her movements are long, similar to those of massage, and not the circular movements she used before.

When the healer completes the entire treatment – about an hour and a half – the patient feels sleepy (and may even fall asleep). In many cases, the sheet is wet with perspiration.

The healer, despite her exhaustion, slowly helps the patient into a sitting position and brings him a glass of water. When he gets off the table, she supports him. (Sometimes, patients feel the need to sit for a few moments following a treatment, mainly to balance their blood pressure. It is therefore advisable to have a mat or a small carpet in the room, and to teach the patient to sit in *cross-legged* on the rug).

The healer accompanies the patient out of the room. If payment is required, this is done outside the treatment room.

This description is, of course, a general outline of a Reiki treatment.

Presently, we will describe certain situations or phenomena which occur during Reiki treatments, and which will eventually be experienced by every healer. First, however, we must clarify one point.

Remember that Reiki *is not harmful.* Hence, during a prolonged Reiki treatment, nothing harmful can possibly happen! Even if seemingly alarming symptoms appear, such as perspiration or trembling, they will not cause any harm. Therefore, a Reiki treatment must be thorough and ongoing in order for it to afford the patient the best possible results.

Now we will examine different situations and treatments which might come up during a Reiki session.

Weeping

A phenomenon which often embarrasses the healer is weeping. It bursts forth suddenly and surprisingly when the healer touches a certain point on the patient's body (mainly around the heart chakra).

It appears as if the patient is crying for no reason at all, but the patient actually has no control over it. This crying must be seen as a channel for purification and cleansing which removes a great blockage from the energy channels. Often, it is accompanied by tears, "which purify the paths of vision," or wailing and groaning, which cleanse phlegm passages.

There is no reason to terminate the treatment if the patient starts crying. The healer must stop moving his hands at the point which provokes the crying (known as the crying trigger, in professional literature) and wait until the crisis passes.

Loss of Bladder Control

Another well-known phenomenon, and even more embarrassing, is the patient's loss of bladder control (particularly with women). Urine leaks on to the sheet or on to the floor, sometimes even forming a small puddle, and on other occasions there is a noisy passing of gas. This phenomenon may appear when the healer's hands are on any part of the patient's body, but mainly when the patient is lying on his side. There is no reason to stop the treatment, except in extreme cases of urine leakage. One must remember that the situation is unpleasant for both the patient and the healer but it does cease after several treatments (and if it recurs, it must be considered a health/ physical problem to be dealt with by a physician).

Heat Waves, Cold Waves, Goose Bumps, Trembling and Tingling

Many phenomena are expressed on the patient's skin: fluctuations in body temperature cause sensations of heat and cold and changes on the surface of the skin. These are natural occurrences which show that the treatment is going well and that the Reiki process has actually begun. Usually, these phenomena disappear after about half an hour. If they continue until the end of the treatment, it indicates that the patient is in a bad way, and a schedule of daily treatments must be planned for the next two weeks.

Bodily Tension

Most healers are aware of the changes in bodily tension. First, the body of the patient becomes rigid and tense, and later the tension disappears and the muscles relax. This is a natural condition.

However, at times the body is relaxed at the beginning of the treatment, and signs of tension – rigid muscles, for example – appear during the treatment. If these signs do not disappear by the end of the treatment, it indicates that there is a problem the Reiki healer has not located.

In cases such as these, the patient should take a hot bath or have a relaxing massage prior to the next treatment.

Changes in the Breathing Rhythm. Wheezing.

We must differentiate between these two similar phenomena. A change in the breathing rhythm is a normal and acceptable occurrence during a Reiki treatment. Usually, breathing changes according to the breathing of the healer, with the patient breathing deeply and steadily. However, occasionally wheezing is heard, and it does not cease within a few seconds.

In cases such as this, the patient must be turned over on his right side and treated until the wheezing ceases.

Asthma Attacks

People suffering from asthma and similar diseases may exhibit signs of asthma attacks during a Reiki treatment session. In such a case, *the treatment must cease.* Treatments may only continue only after the patient has been treated medically – and not the same day.

Rebirth

On occasion, Reiki leads to a phenomenon similar to that known to occur during the experience of rebirth. The individual feels as if he has been reborn, and display signs of "babiness". Many Reiki healers also serve as rebirth instructors, since the two methods are so similar.

Reincarnation

Reiki often leads to a "path" of reincarnation, and both the patient and healer sense past lives. (See the relevant chapter.)

Involuntary Meditation

Reiki leads to situations similar to total meditation. The main phenomena will be flashing lights in front of the patient's eyes, colored lights resembling fireworks, visions, and a sense of "the opening of the chakras". These occurrences are not at all negative.

Changes in Blood Pressure

Reiki may cause changes in the patient's blood pressure. Usually, it is regulating – high blood pressure is lowered and low blood pressure is raised – but one must remember that extreme changes in blood pressure or extreme levels of blood pressure (high or low) require medical attention.

Blurred Vision

Often the patient senses that his vision is blurred following a Reiki treatment. This condition passes about an hour after the treatment.

Side Effects Following Treatment

Treatment is frequently followed by side effects. These must be monitored, and if they do not disappear after three days, the patient should seek medical advice. Amongst the side effects are:

Nausea, biliousness, stomach-aches.

Headaches and migraines.

Muscular weakness.

Increased perspiration, sometimes accompanied by a strong body odor.

Dryness of the mouth.

Frequent urination.

Cloudy urine.

Diarrhea.

An increase of body temperature by up toone degree.

Feelings of depression or sadness.

These side effects do not necessarily appear, but when they do – one or more of them – they appear in moderation.

If one of these side effects appears in an extreme form, medical treatment should be considered. The same goes for a symptom (however slight), that does not disappear after three days.

In conclusion, the Reiki healer must prepare a treatment plan for each patient. Usually, the desirable treatment will take place once every two days over the course of two weeks, and later, one or two treatments each week. It is desirable that the healer prepare the plan at the end of the first meeting and discuss it with the patient.

First-Level Reiki

First-level Reiki teaches one how to treat oneself and others with the laying on of hands. This is the most basic level of Reiki. I will now attempt to describe a typical course, according to a method which I have developed over a number of years.

First-level Reiki must be taught consecutively. The best framework is a weekend gathering, preferably two full days, during which participants attend five instructional sessions and three Reiki treatment/exercise workshops.

In view of the fact that Reiki is taught through initiation, the group should not be too large. I have discovered that a small group – two or three students – makes it more difficult, as a Reiki learning group has a quality of its own and the size of the group determines its quality.

On the other hand, too large a group impairs concentration. The ideal number of participants in each course is six or seven.

Day 1

The First Session

The first session is devoted to the teacher getting to know his students. This goes beyond simple introductions and may include, for example, encouraging students to adjust to the atmosphere of the course by removing their shoes, sitting comfortably, and so on.

After this, the teacher describes the environment in which the Reiki process is supposed to take place (it is important that the course take place in a similar environment). In other words, the teacher presents the basic principles: a quiet, well-lit room, a comfortable treatment table, about as high as a regular table, a candle containing essential oils or incense to create a pleasant aroma, quiet calming music, indirect light – preferably sunlight filtered through a curtain or candlelight – a small pillow under the patient's head, a white sheet, a small basin or bowl for rinsing hands, and a towel to wipe away perspiration. The teacher emphasizes that each healer must first make the treatment environment comfortable for himself, and only then for his patients. If, for example, a healer treats children, he must make the room suitable for children. If he is treating a handicapped person, he must bear his limitations in mind. One healer I met, blind from birth, prepared a treatment room with tiny bells attached to strings hanging from the ceiling, so that, among other things, he would always be able to identify his position in relation to his patient.

After presenting the practical aspects of Reiki, I then give the students a short lecture on the essence of Reiki, emphasizing the fact that Reiki is an immense cosmic energy which already exists within everyone and all around. I explain to the students that Reiki exists in and around them, and that in time, if they follow the necessary initiation steps, it will rise to the surface.

This concludes the first session.

The Second Session

During the second session, the student has his first encounter with the essence of Reiki and his initiation begins.

I usually begin this session by showing each student my bare hands. The students sit in a *crossed-legged position*, eyes partially closed, hands resting on their knees, palms up. The ideal situation is achieved when six students are sitting in a circle around me, and I direct myself to each one in turn.

I usually raise my hands and place my palms on the student's open palms. During this process, I contemplate the specific connection I have with each student. (These connections are not the symbols transmitted to trainees during second level Reiki, which some call "first-level Reiki symbols". As this may cause confusion, we will call them "connections".) This connection is a reaction to what I pick up from the student – his appearance, the rhythm of his breathing, his aura, his body language. After a few moments, I feel the student's palms becoming warm and I know that he is now open to the cosmic Reiki energy and that the energy channel is leading Reiki to him. Usually, at this stage, he straightens his back, raises his chin a little, and tilts his head backwards.

For about a half hour, I pass from one student to the next, until each has experienced his first contact with cosmic Reiki energy. Without pausing, I begin a second round, during which I place my right hand on each student's forehead and my left on the area of his heart. At this point, the students are usually immersed in some kind of meditative state. The connection I transmit is now formulated as a request to the student: "Open your heart to the beauty of Reiki," "Let yourself flow with the light which is emanating from within you," and so on. This time I do not sense waves of heat, but I am strongly aware of the student's physical reaction. Many experience dryness of the mouth and lick their lips. Some blink and move their eyes nervously. They have goose bumps, as if they felt a cold draft, and their nipples (of both men and women) become erect. From time to time, the students let out an involuntarily whimper.

Having completed the second round, I instruct each student to turn to the student on his right and perform the first two steps consecutively: sending Reiki through the palms of his hands and through the upper chakras to the student on his right. In this manner, each student gives and receives the Reiki energy, simultaneously. To begin with, this exercise is done with some degree of clumsiness, but after a while, the Reiki circle closes and the power of the Reiki increases. After ten minutes, each student turns to the left and transmits Reiki energy to the student on the other side.

To conclude the session, I sit in the center of the circle and each one of the students gives Reiki energy to me, thereby enabling me to leave the session strengthened. At the same time, I examine each student in order to sense if the energy channels have been opened inside him and if he has really mastered the first level of Reiki.

The First Workshop

At the end of the first day, the first workshop takes place. Each student enters the treatment room on his own, and I give him a full Reiki treatment, including all the stages. The student lies downs on his back on the treatment table and I first treat the front of his body, then his right side, then his left side, and, finally, his back. A description of a typical Reiki treatment appears in a separate chapter, so I will not repeat it here. However, I will discuss a few important points concerning the first-level Reiki practical session:

1. Remember that the student reaches this stage of the practical session after a day charged with emotion, and he is therefore very sensitive. As a result, there is a good chance he will cry, be hysterical, etc.

2. Remember that the Reiki teacher is tired. This does not effect the Reiki energy, since an experienced teacher becomes stronger throughout the course. Now, at the end of the day, he is overflowing with Reiki energy; but it is important when considering the teacher's physical strength.

3. Remember that a connection between the teacher/ student, the healer (teacher)/patient has already been forged – the initiation. This connection leads to a high degree of intimacy, since both are transmitting energy on the same wave-length. There is an inherent danger of abusing this positive and powerful energy. The intimacy of Reiki is liable to lead to intimacy which is mistakenly expressed through sexuality. On occasion, a female Reiki teacher may

discern such phenomena such as erections amongst male students, while the male teacher might be aware of similar arousal among female students. It is advisable to perform the treatment with the door ajar.

The first two sessions and the workshop conclude the first day of Reiki instruction.

Day 2

The Third Session

The third session, which begins the second day, starts with a few minutes of individual meditation, in which each student attempts to focus his consciousness on his experiences during the first day of instruction. Following the brief meditation, the teacher divides the students into pairs. If there is an uneven number of students, the teacher joins one of the students as a partner. If there is an even number of students, the teacher does not participate in the exercise.

The objective of the session is to learn the basic movements of the treatment (experienced by the students during the first day, in their first workshop) through the opening of all the chakras.

7

We begin with the highest chakra, the seventh or crown chakra. One of the students lies on his back, while his partner kneels behind his head, placing his hands on the eyes of the prostrate student, covering them; the fingers are placed on his cheeks, and the heel of the hand on his forehead. As soon as heat or light is sensed, this is a sign that the chakra has opened to the Reiki energy and the students switch roles.

6

The sixth chakra, the third eye, located in the center of the forehead, is next. In order to open this chakra, we place the palms on the temples, in a parallel position. The opening of this chakra is very rapid.

5

The next chakra is the fifth chakra, the throat chakra. In order to open this chakra, we hold the patient's head in the palms of the hands, at the nape and sides of the neck. Then we raise the head a little and move it gently from right to left, preferably in a circular motion. This treatment must be carried out with great caution and the teacher must supervise the opening of this chakra with great care. Some students will not succeed in opening this chakra and the teacher will have to assist them.

Up to this point, three movements have been carried out with the person performing the Reiki treatment located behind the student, or "patient". From this point on, the healer may move to the patient's side, if he wishes.

4

The fourth chakra is the heart chakra, the basis of any Reiki treatment. In this case, we place the hands over the heart. The direction of the fingers is not important. It is necessary to open this chakra until the healer feels heat and a gentle tickling in his palms. The opening of the heart chakra, even as an exercise, immediately improves breathing.

3

The third chakra is the solar plexus chakra, which is opened by placing the hands over the stomach, from above. The opening of this chakra immediately improves digestion. Sometimes, the opening of this chakra is accompanied by noises in the stomach resembling the sound of waves hitting the sand.

2

The second chakra is the sexual chakra; treating it and opening it occur by sending a flow of Reiki energy to the liver. The hands are placed on each side of the body, beneath the stomach and parallel to the liver. The opening of this chakra frees the patient of profound distress and depression. Following the opening of this chakra, the hands are placed in the area between the navel and the genitals. This treatment improves the individual's sexuality.

1

The first chakra, the base chakra, is the last to receive Reiki treatment. In order to open this chakra, the hands must be placed at the junction between the limbs and the torso, beneath the genitals, with the fingers pointing towards the legs. The best way to perform this treatment is to lean over the patient with legs spread wide, facing the patient's legs. Although at this stage there is a good relationship between the students, and their Reiki energy channels are open, there is a certain degree of embarrassment involved in the opening of this chakra. But it must be treated!

At this point, the students are exhausted. Each has given and received seven treatments. We therefore take a short break.

The Second Workshop

During this workshop, the students switch partners and each member of the couple opens every one of his partner's seven chakras consecutively and sends Reiki energy into them. Only after all the chakras have been opened do they exchange roles.

After this, another short break is taken.

The Fourth Session

The fourth session is devoted to the opening of the chakras, with the patient now lying on his stomach. Treatment is performed from the back. Here, as well, the treatment starts at the head, moving downward. It may be done with the same partners as during the previous session or with new partners, and may be done consecutively, followed by an exchange of roles or an exchange of partners after each chakra.

At this point, the student is at a considerably advanced stage and is able, with the aid of his natural senses which have been strengthened by Reiki, to make the correct choices by himself. Just as Reiki "leads itself" to the place which requires attention, so the student will "lead himself" to the required treatment.

At the end of this stage, the students lie down on their stomachs and I pass from one to the other, performing what is known by teachers as "Reiki lightning." This means transmitting an extremely strong wave of Reiki energy which floods the body like an electric shock. It takes a long time before a Reiki healer is able to deliver such a thorough Reiki energy cleansing. The purpose of "Reiki lightning" is to solve difficult problems or alleviate various states of shock.

In order to create "Reiki lightning," I place my right hand between the buttocks of the student/patient, with the thumb pressing on the small indentation above the anus, between the buttocks. The left hand is placed on the nape of the student's neck, with the thumb pressing on the central depression. In this position, I transmit Reiki energy, as well as two additional connections, creating the connection between teacher and student. In the first connection, I relate to the student himself, personally, while in the second, I present the student with the name by which he will refer to me in his thoughts (a name that might change from student to student, but not necessarily).

When I finish transmitting "Reiki lightning" to all the students, the session is over. In practice, every student is now certified to give Reiki treatments.

[At this point, I find it necessary to comment on a matter which will be discussed at another point in the book. Many Reiki teachers treat the symbols transmitted during the second level of Reiki – symbolic images originating in the East – as cosmic symbols, common to all humanity. During the second-level Reiki course, the student learns to draw these symbols and receives them consciously. During the first-level Reiki course, the teacher outlines the symbols with his finger at the base of the student's spine, thus "imprinting" the symbols, without the student being aware of it. When the teacher does this, the "connections" we have spoken of are not necessary, and the Reiki symbols – three or four of them – will be imprinted upon the students during the last stage of the course. I myself believe, as does my teacher, that the pool of Reiki symbols is extremely broad, almost endless, and the symbols may assume the form of a word, emblem, drawing, sound or sentence. The universality of the symbols is a result of the Reiki energy itself, and the symbol, on its own, is only a symbol.]

The Third Workshop

During the third workshop, the students give each other treatment. They must attempt to perform the treatment on the sides of the body on their own.

All couples work simultaneously, with the teacher moving from pair to pair, correcting and offering assistance, where necessary. If there are patients on hand, the students may attempt to give them treatment them under the teacher's supervision.

The Fifth Session

This is the last meeting of the first-level Reiki course.

During this session, I review different points, demonstrating them with the help of the students. These points might change from course to course, depending on how the earlier meetings went. (If we encounter a certain problem, I immediately explain its consequences.) However, it usually includes the following:

1. An explanation of the situation in which the palms of the hands "adhere" to the body. This is a vacuum-like situation, whereby the patient has no Reiki in the area beneath his palms, and a vacuum is created, drawing the Reiki into him. If this happens, the area will require a long and thorough treatment.

2. An explanation regarding the situation in which extreme heat is experienced – an excess of Reiki in the form of a whirlpool has been transmitted. The patient must be treated until the flow and the heat have been stabilized.

3. An explanation of the situation in which extreme cold is experienced – a lack of Reiki. An energy block.

4. Pain in the palms of the hands – resulting from pain in the patient's body in the area which the healer is touching. This area must be given immediate and lengthy treatment!

5. A tingling or prickling sensation in the palms – indicates that the Reiki energy is working!

6. A feeling of electric shock – indicates that the treatment opened a central Reiki channel (usually a chakra) that was blocked for a long time. Continue the treatment, as this signifies "barren earth", which requires intensive Reiki.

During the second part of the session, I explain and demonstrate to the students how one may perform a Reiki treatment on oneself, or more specifically, how I treat myself. The principle is similar to that of treating another person. However, the position of the palms of the hands must be adapted to self-treatment, particularly in the area of the back. At the end of the demonstration, each student gives himself a short Reiki treatment.

That's it! The first level Reiki course has ended. I once again reiterate my warning to the now certified students against using Reiki for negative purposes, direct them to learning materials which will help them develop and advance on their path, and restate the Reiki principles in the form of a brief motto ("Do not be angry", "Do not worry", and so on). I also present each of them with a diploma stating that they are now certified Reiki healers of the first level.

And since I believe that each additional Reiki healer – each trainee who offers and gives Reiki – contributes both to his environment and to the entire world, I feel that I have fulfilled my responsibility to the universe, to society, to my esteemed teacher, and to myself.

Second-Level Reiki

Having completed first-level Reiki training and spent a certain amount of time practicing the receiving and giving of Reiki – in other words, self-treatment and treating others, the student is now ready to begin the next stage – second-level Reiki.

First-level Reiki is characterized by the laying on of hands, which completes an energy circuit and transmits Reiki energy. Removal of the hands cuts the flow of Reiki energy. In addition to this situation, which requires physical contact between the therapist and the patient, first-level Reiki is predominantly aimed at healing and treating physical problems, and is only marginally devoted to spiritual and emotional problems.

After sufficient time has passed (at least two weeks from the end of first-level Reiki certification, but preferably even more), the student may participate in a course which teaches second-level Reiki.

Second-level Reiki is spiritual Reiki. It is done by sending Reiki energy to a certain target which is not necessarily in close physical proximity to the healer. Moreover, it is not mandatory for the healer and the patient to make each other's acquaintance, as it is in first-level Reiki. To a certain degree, it resembles sending sound waves into space, and anyone who wishes to listen, can do so. However, when it comes to Reiki, we usually attach a certain "code" which directs the Reiki energy to the particular patient.

Second-level Reiki is therefore "long-distance Reiki", which works not with physical contact, but with spiritual/ mental contact. This type of Reiki works both on the physical level and the spiritual level, and is very effective in areas such as reincarnation, astral travel and helping to make "wishes" come true, as well as in communicating with animals and mother earth (the whole of nature) in general.

Second-level Reiki works when the healer focuses his mind on the *target* to which he is sending Reiki energy (for example, a sick person or someone in another country), and transmits the energy through his thoughts. The "messenger" transmitting Reiki energy is the symbol which the student receives during the process of second-level Reiki training. The transmitted Reiki energy is very powerful, more so than that transmitted with the laying on of hands.

[Incidentally, when the student participates in second-level Reiki initiation, his ability to treat and cure using first-level Reiki increases, at times significantly.]

Symbols are a complex subject in the theory of Reiki. I, like my esteemed teacher, do not agree with most Reiki teachers regarding the nature of these symbols. I will present the different opinions below.

The majority of Reiki teachers believe that the symbols, which are holy and secret, are universal. In other words, there are a number of sacred symbols (usually three to five) which the teacher transmits to the student in two stages: during first-level Reiki initiation, unconsciously, by outlining them on the student's back, and later, during second-level Reiki initiation, by the student's conscious study of the symbol's shape.

The symbols, which are graphic shapes, are drawn on a piece of paper and the student must copy and learn them, as the papers are destroyed after each lesson (burnt or buried). In addition, the student memorizes the name of the symbol.

A students wishing to send Reiki energy by means of a symbol, "invites" the symbol into his awareness by creating an image of the symbol in his mind, or by contemplating the sound of the symbol's name, thereby charging it with the Reiki energy and transmitting it to the objective.

The sacred symbols are universal (in other words, each second-level Reiki student receives at least some of them) and confidential. In the opinion of many Reiki teachers, the most closely guarded secret is the knowledge of the symbols, and anyone who reveals their essence would be considered a traitor and ostracized by the community of Reiki instructors.

I learned a different approach to the symbols from my teacher, Master Naharo. The symbols, according to his understanding, can be almost anything that awakens an association or image of the symbol in the student's mind, such as images of living creatures. I may decide that my symbol is a bird, charge it with Reiki energy, and send it to its destination. But even with this method, the student receives the symbols from his teacher – four symbols chosen by the teacher for his student, depending on what feeling he has about him, and an additional symbol, one of the teacher's personal symbols, transmitted from teacher to student.

Thus, for example, the student may be given the symbol of a cloud, a turtle, a Star of David, "Ahhhmmm", yellow.

The first is taken from nature, the second is an animal, the third is an important graphic shape, the fourth a sound, and the fifth a color. When he wants to transmit

Reiki energy, he intuitively selects the most appropriate symbol and sends it via Reiki.

The master transfers the symbols to the students during a course or workshop mainly dedicated to practice (since the students are already familiar with Reiki). Practice begins by the transmission of Reiki between the people present, *without touching*, to be sure it works. It continues by sending the Reiki energy far away, to individuals either known or unknown to the student. At least one exercise must involve a group Reiki transmission (with everyone participating), all focusing on a single target. Another involves each student sending Reiki randomly to an undefined group (for instance, to headache sufferers throughout the world).

During second-level Reiki, the healer transmitting Reiki energy frequently holds his hands in front of his chest, as if repelling a heavy object. This is an accepted and favored position. Moreover, some healers close their eyes while sending Reiki energy. This is also accepted practice.

Remember that since Reiki is harmless, there is no need to ask the patient's permission in order to send second-level Reiki (unlike treatment with the palm of the hand). You can, for example, send Reiki to every single patient in a particular hospital, without having to ask their permission. Such acts also serve to reinforce the practitioner's ability to concentrate and send Reiki, and is an excellent form of practice.

First-level Reiki is never performed without payment or some kind of remuneration. This is one of the practical principles of Reiki: a person does not value something obtained for nothing, and the Reiki healer should therefore charge an appropriate fee so that the wonderful gift of Reiki will be valued.

The only occasion when Reiki may be offered without payment is when second-level Reiki is sent "to the whole world" or to an unknowing target, or when healers voluntarily treat animals.

Second-level Reiki is excellent for distant healing. I myself receive about ten phone calls a day, and respond by sending Reiki energy to different locations worldwide. Since Reiki is very potent, I need only dedicate a few minutes to each transmission/treatment, whereas first-level Reiki requires a treatment of at least an hour.

Second-level Reiki is extremely powerful when performed in a group and has far greater power than that sent individually by each member of the group. Moreover, members of the group can be in different locations around the world. If everybody sends Reiki to the *same target* at the *same instant*, it is considered group Reiki and has tremendous power.

As noted before, second-level Reiki is good for all kinds of mental and spiritual treatment and healing. Research has shown that spiritual and emotional problems are far more difficult to treat than physical ones. Furthermore, treatment on the spiritual and mental levels *invariably* improves the physical condition.

Let me repeat: Second-level Reiki is a superb way to communicate with and treat animals. Try it with an animal in your vicinity and see its effectiveness for yourself.

Another advantage of second-level Reiki is that it can affect a person's future. Say, for example, someone needs to pass an examination in a week's time; he can ask the Reiki healer to send Reiki energy to his future, or he can do it himself. The healer then pictures the problem, forms the image of the patient "passing the test" in his mind using guided imagery, then sends the Reiki energy. Surprisingly, it works much more often than one would imagine!

I will conclude this section with three personal stories:

A year ago, while in London, I experienced a strange sense of distress. The image of a good friend of mine, who at the time was in New Orleans on business, kept coming to mind. I decided to send him second-level Reiki, and did this for twenty minutes. Only two weeks later did I learn that my friend had been involved in a traffic accident and had been seriously injured at exactly the time I had experienced the sense of distress. When we next met, he told me that while in hospital, he felt waves of heat passing through his body and thought that he could see me! He recovered completely.

A year ago, a well-known and colorful NBA football player became involved in physical fights in almost every game he played – much to the dismay of his coach and the team management, and to the delight of the opposing teams. One of the owners of the team, who knew me, set me a simple task (accompanied by a sizable fee). As a result, I found myself watching every basketball game shown on TV for an entire year, and sending soothing Reiki energy to the basketball court. That year, only two violent incidents occurred involving this player – and in both cases, players from the opposing team initiated the fight. The player himself had no idea of my role in the games.

Finally, a personal note. Many years ago, when I was a boy, I had a small dog, a mongrel, that was my best and closest friend throughout childhood. When the dog died, I buried him in my parents' garden and mourned him for a long time. About thirty years later, I started wondering if I would ever enjoy the friendship of a four-legged creature again. I began to send visual Reiki energy, picturing myself with the dog that had filled my childhood with so much joy. Three months after performing the Reiki, I discovered a puppy abandoned in my yard. That puppy is the dog that is curled up at my feet as I write, and accompanies me wherever I go.

The Hidden Secrets of Reiki

To those interested in Reiki, it seems that Reiki's secret lies in the symbols, the enigmatic signs passed first by means of initiation, from Master to student, emanating consciously from the teacher and absorbed unconsciously by the student.

Finally, in second-level Reiki, they are transmitted to the student in a conscious fashion.

This, however, is not the hidden secret of Reiki.

The hidden secret of Reiki, the secret used by the experienced Reiki healer to treat almost everyone, whatever his affliction, is much more straightforward than this:

It is *Marma*.

Marma was defined by scholars of Chinese and Indian medicine in days gone by as points which provide the maximal contact between the physical body and the astral bodies which convey cosmic energy.

Marma points may be described as open channels, appearing in different locations in the body, where one opening is open to cosmic energy and another to the human body. Along the length of each channel are minute perforations which convey cosmic energy throughout the person's body – physical or ethereal.

The Marma points, about 52 in all, form the basis of the entire meridian network and all the acupuncture/pressure/massage points used in alternative medicine.

However, the ability of the Reiki expert to make the most of these points is far greater than in any other technique; he opens the connecting channel, and the Reiki energy flows through into the correct place, in the right quantity and potency, healing the body and mind in the particular area 'controlled' by the Marma point.

Many Reiki teachers are displeased that I am divulging this valuable information to anyone who reads this book.

I actually did deliberate a great deal about this issue, but finally the orders of my esteemed teacher, who taught me the Marma points and instructed me to disseminate the knowledge, overcame my reluctance:

"Reiki is everyone's property and no one has the right to keep the information to himself," he instructed me.

I therefore offer the full list of Marma points, describing their location in the body, the English transliteration of their Sanskrit names (I learned these names in India) and the area controlled by the point.

Remember that there is pairing and parallelism between the body's Marma points: A point on the right arm has an equivalent point on the left arm. A point appearing on one side of the spinal column will appear on the other side, in the identical position and at the same distance from the spine.

1. The point located between the lower and middle thumb phalanges, at the junction of the thumb with the palm, is the **Kshipra** point. It controls passion and spiritual will power during the day, and the stomach, on the physical level, during the night.

2. The point on the palm of the hand, on the mound located beneath the pinkie, is the **Kshiprai** point. It controls passion and spiritual will power during the night, and the stomach, on the physical level, during the day.

3. The point found precisely in the center of the palm, that is, two points, one at the center of the palm of each hand, is the **Talhridaya** point which is directly connected to the heart.

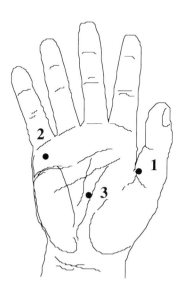

4. Five points, one at the end of each finger (ten points in all for both hands), are referred to as a single point. These are known as the **Talhridayass** points and are linked to the nervous system.

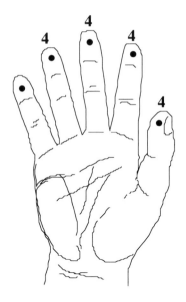

5. The point found on the joint of the hand, beneath the thumb, at the place where the pulse is measured, is known as **Manibandha.** It is most important since it indicates an individual's capacity to express and make the most of his potential in the world. It is the main spiritual indicator in every Reiki treatment.

6. The point found on the hand joint, parallel to point 5 but beneath the pinkie, is called **Koorchsha** and is responsible for blood circulation.

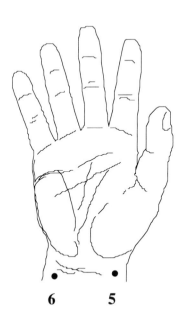

6   **5**

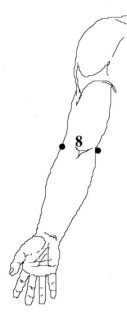

7. The point found on the arm, in the inner crease of the elbow joint, is known as **Karpooram** and is the main point connected to vitality and sexual energy.

8. **Two** points (on each arm), located on either side of the elbow, are known as **Kurpara** and are responsible for the liver, the urinary tract and the pancreas.

9. The point found on the outside of the arm, halfway between the elbow and the shoulder, is known as **Oorvi** and is responsible for the blood flow rate.

10. **Two** points at the back of the neck, separated by the two finger-widths (of the particular person), are called **Kraknrik** and are responsible for the heart chakra (opening and closing), the lungs and the chest. These are important points in every Reiki treatment.

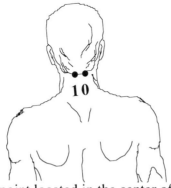

11. **One** point located in the center of the skull, at the back, facing the third eye chakra, is known as the upper **Kraknrik**. It is an important point, responsible for allergies, depression and low spirits, which some ignore due to the difficulty in treating it.

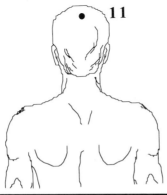

12. **Two** points situated on the neck, at the front, under the ears, are the well known **Manya** which are responsible for the blood capillaries and blood flow through the secondary blood vessels (that is, not veins and arteries).

13. **Two** points at the base of the neck are the well known **Shamantrika**, points which are responsible for the main blood vessels – the aorta, arteries and veins.

14. **One** point located at the bottom of the lower triangle of the neck, between the bones is the important **Neela** point which is responsible for the fifth chakra and the thyroid gland.

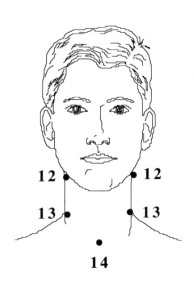

15. **One** point (it has no parallel on the opposite side of the body) in the upper left section of the chest, beneath the lateral bone, in a straight line down from the left ear, is the **Apastamgh** point. This is connected to muscle action, including that of the heart, and is treated in cases of muscle tension.

16. **One** point exactly parallel to point number 15, but on the right side of the chest is the important **Kakshadhara** point. This is also associated with muscular activity, including that of the heart, treated in cases of muscle slackness.

17. **One** point located exactly in the center of the chest, on the line connecting the armpits, is the **Hridayam** point, responsible for the fourth chakra and the thymus gland.

18. **One** point located a finger-width below point 17, is the lower **Hridayam** point which is directly connected to the heart.

19. **One** point located five finger-widths below point 18 is the well-known **Manipura** point which is in charge of the third chakra and human will power.

20. **One** central point located beneath the navel, three finger-widths below, is the **Nabi** point. This is one of the most important points in Reiki and is responsible for the second chakra (sexual), physical and emotional equilibrium, human creativity, judgment and drawing conclusions.

21. **One** point located above the groin is known as **Vasth.** It is the main point for everything concerning sexual ability, in the sense of fertility and fertilization and ability to reproduce, and is a very important point in Reiki.

22. **One** point located in the center of the groin (in men a little more to the left) is known as **Lohitaksham.** This point is responsible for the lymphatic system.

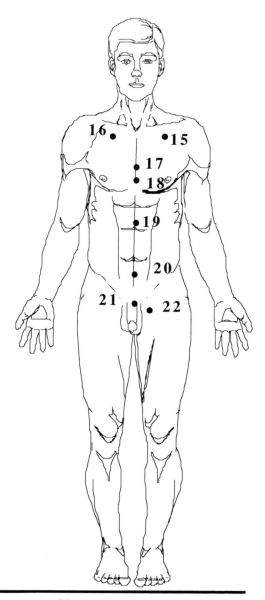

23. The point located in the center of the front of the thigh (in both thighs) is known as **Oovi** and is responsible for walking (and in the spiritual sense, for an individual to advance toward his/her goals).

24. The point located three finger-widths above the knee, known as **Ani**, is responsible for balance.

25. **Two** points (on each knee), one exactly above the center front of the knee, the other parallel to it on the inside of the knee, are the upper **Janu** points. They are responsible for balance (both physical and spiritual).

26. **Two points** (on each knee), one exactly below the center front of the knee, the other parallel to it on the inside of the knee, are the lower **Janu** points and are responsible for the joints in the body.

27. The point in the center of the shin, halfway between the knee and the ankle, is the **Januara** point and is responsible for the kidneys and the flow of adrenaline in the body.

28. The point located on the inner side of the shin, seven finger-widths from the ankle, is known as the upper **Gulpha** point, and is an important point in the male reproductive system.

29. **Two** points located on the ankle, one at the front, the second on the inner side, are the lower **Gulpha** points, responsible for the female reproductive system.

(We should stress that in Reiki, points 28 and 29 are treated jointly for both male and female reproductive problems).

30. **Five** points, located at the junctions of the toes with the foot, are the **Khipram** points, responsible for the sinuses and to some extent the lymphatic system.

31. The point located on the sole of the foot, in the middle of the mound beneath the big toe, is known as **Koorcha** and is responsible for the stomach. It is an important point in Reiki and a central point in reflexology.

32. The point located on the sole of the foot, in the groove in the center of the foot, is known as **Talhridayam** and is directly connected to the heart.

33. The point located on the sole of the foot, in the center of the ankle, is the famous **Koorchshir** and is responsible for the first chakra.

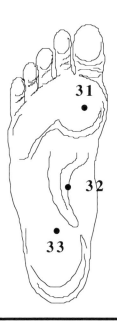

34. The point located at the center of the shin, at the back, eight finger-widths from the ankle, is the lower **Indravastih** point. It is responsible for athletic ability (the ability to operate muscles rapidly and with full power).

35. The point located five finger-widths above point 34, at the center of the shin at the back, is the upper **Indravastih** point. It is responsible for muscle contraction (or pain in the limbs, mostly the feet).

36. The point located behind the knee, at the center, is called **Janu** and is an extremely important point. It controls the function of the liver, the urinary tract and the spleen, and is a central point in every Reiki treatment.

37. The point located at the back of the thigh, five finger-widths above the knee crease, is the well known **Aanih** point and is linked to the genital organs.

38. The point located at the upper back of the thigh, two finger-widths below the junction of the buttock and thigh, is the **Vorvee** point which deals particularly with blood circulation in the legs.

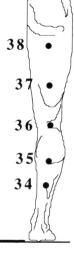

39. **Two** points located in the center of the buttocks, known as **Kteektaninam**, are key points in achieving physical, emotional and spiritual equilibrium (including sense of balance). They are an important part of any Reiki treatment.

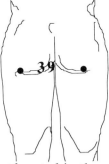

40. **One** point located in the upper zone of the ridge between the buttocks, where a small hollow can be felt, is the famous **Gudam** and is directly linked to the first chakra.

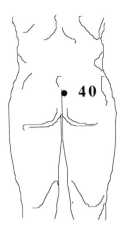

41. **Two** points located
five finger-widths above point
40 and two finger-widths from
the spine (in each direction) are
the **Kukundaraye** points
which are linked to the second
chakra.

42. **Two** points located
five finger-widths above point
41, and four finger-widths
from the spine in each
direction, are the **Nitamba**
points. They are associated
with kidney function.

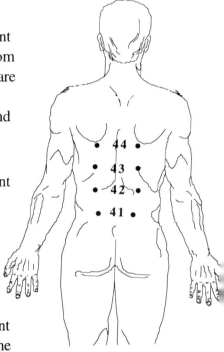

43. **Two** points located
five finger-widths above point
42, the same distance from the
spine, are the **Koopram**
points. They are responsible
for adrenaline balance in the
body.

44. **Two** points on the
lower section of the shoulder-
blades, five finger-widths from
the spine, are the **Vrahti**
points, associated with the
heart and lungs.

45. **Two** points located on the upper section of the shoulder-blades, above point 44, are the **Asphalakah,** associated with the thymus gland and the heart.

46. The point located at the top edge of the shoulder, about a finger-width from the end, is the famous **Asaha** point, associated with the nervous system.

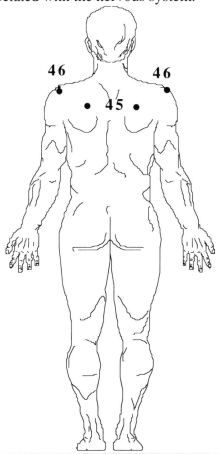

47. The point located above the ear, toward the eye (at the temple) on the skull, is the **Shaunkh** point associated with hearing (not only in the physical sense, but also in the spiritual sense).

48. A point located above the ear toward the back of the neck ("shadow of the ear") on the skull, is the **Utkshepau** point that regulates brain function and is important in any state of increased awareness or enlightenment.

49. The point located at the center of the temple, known as the **Apa,** is directly linked to sight, not just in the physical sense but primarily in the spiritual sense. It is important in all Reiki treatment.

50. The point located in the middle of the brow (above the hair line), is the **Sthapui,** which is linked to the fifth chakra.

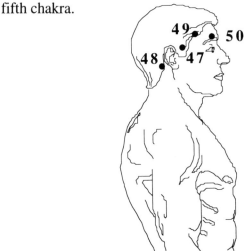

51. A point located at the center of the top of the skull, at the junction of the skull bones (where the fontanelle is visible in a baby's skull), is the **Adhipati** which balances the seventh chakra and is very important in developing an individual's spiritual awareness.

52. A point at the center of the back of the head, on top, before the downward slope of the skull begins, is the **Nadi**, which is responsible for posture.

Please note that the 52 points can overlap. This means, therefore, that an organ, system or problem of a medical/spiritual nature may be treated using different treatment positions (with the patient lying on his back or stomach, and so on).

If you are inexperienced in using Marma points, I recommend placing the entire palm of your hand on the point you wish to treat and transmitting the Reiki in this fashion. If you are experienced, the most effective treatment is to place the cushion of the thumb on the desired point. When there are two points, use both thumbs. When there is only one point, put your thumbs together on the point and direct the Reiki towards it.

The Division of the Body according to Reiki

The First Division

The Division of the Body according to the Chakras (Energy Centers)

This division is meant to lead mainly to physical, spiritual and mental equilibrium by means of a balance of and between the chakras.

The Seventh (Crown) Chakra or **Sahasrara** is responsible for connecting us with our spiritual selves. It controls our upper brain and our right eye. In the endocrine system, the Crown Chakra is responsible for the pituitary gland, a hormone-producing gland at the base of the brain which affects growth.

The Sixth (Third Eye) Chakra or **Ajna** is our intuitive center; in addition, this is where human will and clairvoyance reside. The Third Eye Chakra is responsible for the functioning of the autonomic nervous system (that is, the system of nerve fibres, innervating muscles, glands, etc., whose actions are automatic) and the hypothalamus, as well as the pineal gland, an upgrowth from the optic thalami of the brain.

The Fifth (Throat) Chakra or **Vishudda** is responsible for communication, self-expression and clairaudience (that is, the power of hearing things not present to the senses), as well as for the functioning of throat and lungs. In the endocrine system, the Throat Chakra rules the thyroid, a ductless gland situated in the neck, which regulates metabolism.

The Fourth (Heart) Chakra or **Anahata** governs the emotions of love and compassion. It is responsible for the functioning of heart, lungs, liver and circulatory system. In the endocrine system, the Heart Chakra is responsible for the thymus, a ductless gland at the base of the neck.

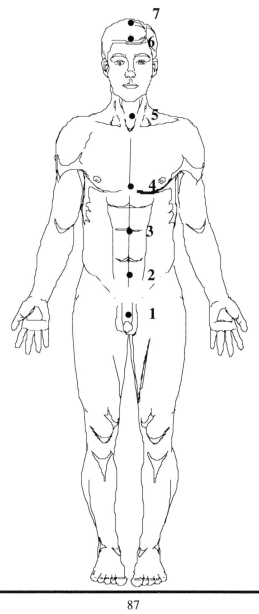

The Third (Solar Plexus) Chakra or **Manipura** is our power and wisdom center. It is responsible for the functioning of stomach, liver and gall-bladder - the digestive system. In the endocrine system, the Solar Plexus Chakra governs the adrenal glands, which are situated beside the kidneys and secrete adrenaline.

The Second (Sacral or Splenic) Chakra or **Svadhisthana** is the center for sexual energy, as well as for emotions and feelings. The Sacral Chakra is responsible for the functioning of the reproductive organs, as well as of the gonads - the organs that produce sex cells - in the endocrine system.

The First (Base) Chakra or **Muladhara** is where survival issues, physical vitality, creative expression and abundance issues reside; it is also the seat of Kundalini. The Base Chakra is responsible for the functioning of the kidneys, bladder and spine. In the endocrine system, it governs the suprarenal glands, which are situated above the kidneys.

The Second Division

The Division of the Body According to its Parts

This division characterizes each part of the body and its connection to the chakras, feelings, and so on.

There is also a secondary division, according to: head, front torso, limbs and back torso.

The Head:

The **face** is used to express the various facets of our personality.

The **ears** enable us to hear. In addition, they contain acupuncture points for every area of the body.

The **forehead** is an indication of intellectual expression.

The **brow** is our intuitive center, as well as an indication of emotional expression.

The **eyes** show how we perceive the world; nearsightedness means that a person is more withdrawn, while farsightedness implies less inner orientation.

The **nose** is related to the heart because of its coloration and bulbousness. It is the source of our sense of smell, and is connected to sexual response. The nose characterizes self-recognition.

The **mouth** is concerned with survival and security

issues. Through it, we take in nourishment - as well as new ideas.

The **jaw** indicates fear or ease of expression. If it is tense, it signifies a blockage of emotional and verbal communication.

The **neck** is the place where thought and emotions come together. If there is stiffness there, it is due to withheld statements.

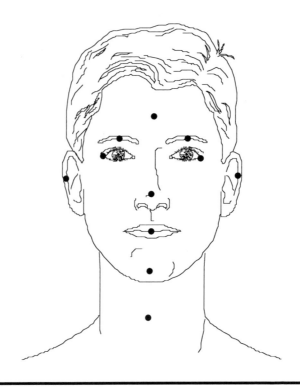

The Front Torso:

The **chest** is involved in relationship issues. It houses the heart and the emotions of love. It is responsible for respiration and circulation.

The **solar plexus** (diaphragm) is the seat of power issues, and those of emotional control. It is also the center for power and wisdom.

The **abdomen** is the seat of the emotions, and contains our deepest feelings. Moreover, it is the center of sexuality, and controls the digestive system.

The **genitals** are related to the Base Chakra containing Kundalini energy (spiritually transformative energy); they are responsible for survival issues, and for a fear of life.

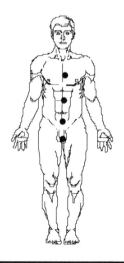

The Limbs:

The **arms and hands** are extensions of the heart center, and express love and emotion.

The **hands** are involved with giving and receiving, with holding on to reality, with reaching goals and with fear of action.

The **arms** express the heart center and love; they enable us to move and connect in the external world.

The **upper arm** gives us the strength to act, and expresses the fear of being discouraged.

The **elbow** connects the strength of the upper arm to the action of the forearm.

The **forearm** is a means of attaining goals, and expresses the fear of inferiority.

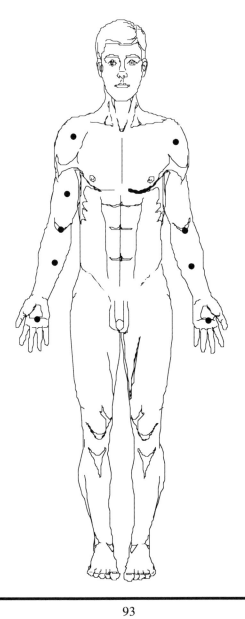

The **thighs** are involved with personal strength, with trust in one's own abilities, as well as the fear of inadequate strength.

The **abductor muscles** in the inner thighs contain sexually charged issues.

The **knees** relate to the fear of death, the fear of the death of the old-self or ego, and the fear of change.

The **lower leg** allows movement toward goals and expresses the fear of action.

The **hamstrings** contain issues of self-control and letting go.

The **ankles** create balance.

The **feet** indicate whether we are grounded. They are connected with reaching our goals, and indicate a fear of completion.

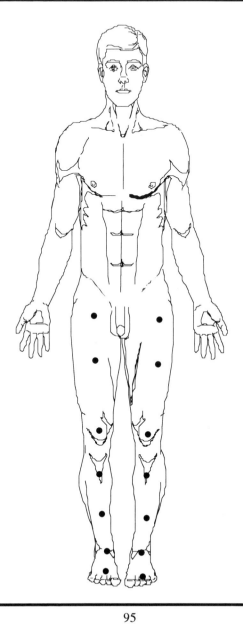

The Back Torso:

The **shoulders** are where we carry the weight of the world; they express the fear of responsibility. Women store a lot on the shoulders.

The **back** is where we store all of our unconscious emotions and excess tension.

The **upper back** is where we carry stored anger - especially between the shoulder-blades.

The **lower back** is the junction between lower and upper body movement. Men store a lot here as a result of the storing of emotions in the belly.

The **pelvis** is the seat of Kundalini energy and the root of basic survival needs and actions.

The **gluteus muscles** are involved in holding in emotion, not releasing and letting to. They are responsible for anal blockage.

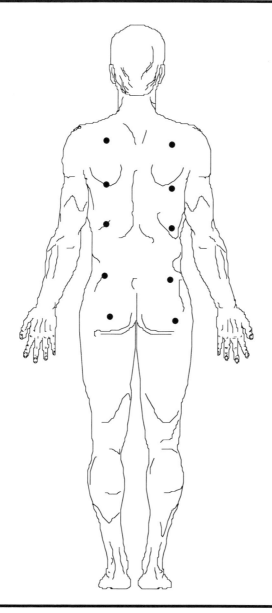

The Third Division

The Division of the Body According to Front and Back

The body is divided up laterally, into a front half and a back half.

Front:

This is our mirror to the world; it contains the emotional issues of daily life such as love, desire, sadness, joy, concern, and so on. Heart "pain" is stored in the chest, between the ribs and the insides of the shoulders. A lot of emotion is also stored in the belly.

Back:

Many of our unconscious thoughts and emotions are stored here. This is where we conceal issues we are not prepared to handle. It is our emotional disposal area for all the things we are not willing to acknowledge. A lot of fear and anger is stored between the shoulder-blades and along the spinalis muscle on either side of the spine.

The Fourth Division

The Division of the Body According to Right and Left

The body is divided up into a left and a right side.

The Right Side:

This is the masculine side, and it is rational, logical, assertive. It is the Yang, and contains the male aspects of the character. It holds anger.

The Left Side:

This is the feminine side, and it is intuitive, receptive, passive. It is the Yin, and contains the female aspects of the character. It holds sadness.

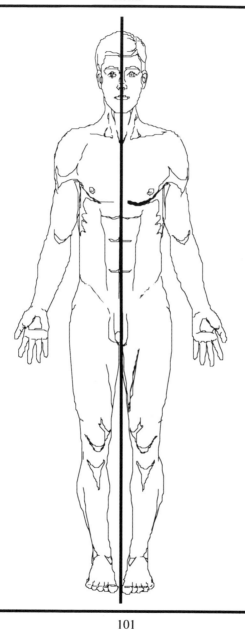

The Fifth Division

The Division of the Body According to Head and Body

In this division, every part has different characteristics.

The Head:

This is characterized by human, mind, intellect and reason.

The Body:

This is characterized by animal, body, feelings and intuition.

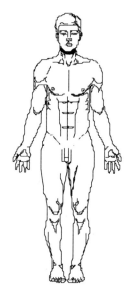

The Sixth Division

The Division of the Body According to Top and Bottom

In this division, the body is divided into two, according to the area above the waist and the area below the waist.

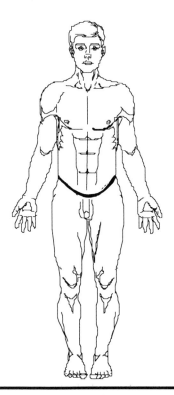

Small Top - Large Bottom:

This is found most often in females. It indicates difficulty in socializing, in outward expression, in interpersonal communications, in self-assertion and taking action. It shows a tendency toward privacy, and characteristics of stability, love of the home and well-groundedness. It is a sign of a passive personality.

Large Top - Small Bottom:

This is found most often in males. It indicates an overdeveloped ability to be assertive, social, expressive and extroverted. It shows a lack of strength and courage with respect to emotional stability and support. It is a sign of an active personality.

The Seventh Division

The Division of the Body According to Limbs and Torso

This divides the body into the limbs and the torso, which includes the head and genitals.

Limbs:

These are our tools for making contact with the outside world. They allow us to move in space, and are the most active parts of the body with regard to the outside world.

Torso:

This is the "core" of the body, the center of the private self. It is very inactive regarding the outside world, and tends to be more reflective, focused on the self.

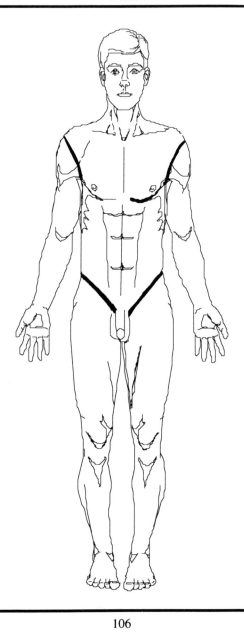

Reiki and Reincarnation

Many Reiki healers are surprised when, in the middle of a routine treatment, they see strange images that do not belong to the time and place in which they are operating. Even more strange, in discussions following the treatment, they discover that their patients saw the same strange images!

It is important to note the importance of discussion following treatment, even though this subject digresses from the main topic of this chapter. During my studies in the Far East, and particularly in India, I was repeatedly surprised to see that during private treatments, the greatest masters devoted almost a quarter of the time to a preliminary discussion with the patient, and even more time to discussion following the treatment.

At first, this seemed to me to be a waste of time. Each day, Master Naharo received about eight to ten individuals for private treatment, and rejected tens of others. As a Westerner, it seemed "wasteful", not because of the loss of contributions or donations to the Master's small income, but because by turning away tens of patients, the basic premise of Reiki – "Do as much good as you can for as many people as you meet" – was being negated!

"When you plant a fruit tree sapling, you must first be familiar with the soil," Master Naharo explained to me, in his colorful way. "You must choose the location, weed the area and dig a small, suitable hole in the ground. This is the preliminary discussion. Following this stage, you plant the sapling. This is the treatment itself. And finally, you pack the soil and give the sapling water and fertilizer; this is the discussion following the treatment. Without all three stages, the tree will not bear fruit."

When I began treatments myself, I followed this three-stage method, and it proved to be wonderfully effective. In many cases, the talks following the treatment taught me new things that I had not been aware of beforehand.

One of the strangest and most interesting phenomena is the appearance of images or segments of life, which appear in front of the healer's eyes during treatment. I remember one case, about two years ago, in which I treated a man suffering from serious pain in his right hand, pains whose origin could not be explained medically. In the middle of the Reiki treatment, I suddenly saw an image of a large wooden bridge, upon which stood a man, almost completely naked. His right hand was attached to the wooden rail with a large iron nail, and blood was flowing from the open wound. When I rose higher in the air (i.e., I reached a higher point of observation, allowing me a greater span of vision), I observed a crowd of people standing near the bridge. All of a sudden the image disappeared.

After the treatment, I told the patient about my vision. He became quite pale and almost collapsed. It seemed that he had seen a similar vision and that the image had appeared several times in his dreams.

A day later, the patient returned, and together we tried to interpret the strange vision. Following a Reiki treatment in which I focused on the vision (as opposed to a specific treatment), we discovered that the image concerned the individual's past; in other words, a former lifetime that he had experienced in another incarnation.

During one of his incarnations, probably two lifetimes ago, he was accused of theft and the penalty was being nailed to the rail of a bridge for an entire day. The pain and the *karma* from the past life were causing the discomfort in his hand in this lifetime. In the end, reconstructing the incarnation led to the disappearance of his pain.

Reiki is indeed an appropriate and effective tool in all issues relating to reincarnation, and as I understand it, Reiki is much more helpful than hypnosis, rebirth or other mystical methods.

Master Naharo, my first and esteemed teacher, was able to enter a total state of meditation. In this state, the Reiki energy, which directs cosmic energy to human beings, creates a passage or bridge between the individual and the enormous aggregation of experiences which have accumulated in the consciousness of the universe. *Thus, a person who is in an appropriate state of meditation and performs Reiki simultaneously, can glimpse the tremendous pool of cosmic consciousness.*

Master Naharo, when in the highest meditative state, is not only able to visit this enormous pool of consciousness (as I also do, on occasion), but also has the rare ability to find his way in this maze of consciousness. In other words, he can follow this massive aggregation of experiences, which resembles billions and billions and billions of piles of straw – each person's and his own reincarnations being a single piece of straw! Only great masters have this ability.

And even so, during a Reiki treatment, a small window is opened, through which the individual is directed by an unseen hand to some segment or other of his past lives. And since the healer and the patient are connected by a channel of energy during the treatment, they can both see the same image at the same time, although not in quite the same manner.

What do I really mean? I will explain my intention by describing an experience I once had. Often, during a Reiki treatment, I find that I see an image of some animal in front of my eyes – a bear, an eagle, a lion, a horse, etc. Clearly, the image of the animal is deeply related to the patient, since each person has an image which accompanies his *karma* and reincarnations. In many cases, it involves the image of a person, family member, great teacher, or the like, who serves as a "mentor" for the individual throughout his different incarnations. Similarly, it may involve an image of a certain animal which plays the role of the person's spiritual "mentor."

The Reiki Master is not always able to make a connection between the image of the animal and the image or sensation that the patient experiences. In one case involving a young woman belonging to the Korean community in San Francisco, I clearly saw the image of a royal eagle gliding at a great altitude with spread wings. At the same time, the patient felt a strong sensation of dizziness and nausea. Later in the treatment, it became clear that she suffered from severe vertigo (fear of heights). Reconstructing her past lives revealed that in one of her incarnations, she had been punished by incarceration in a high tower, and in an attempt to escape, had fallen and broken her neck.

In another case, the image of a small donkey climbing a steep mountain kept on appearing. It turned out that the patient, a Hispanic man (and a wonderfully talented baseball player), had been, in one of his past lives, a slave who worked on the wharves, loading and unloading heavy building blocks.

Many people do not believe in reincarnation, particularly in the West. Even amongst those who have been attracted to the wonders of Reiki, many see it as an alternative health treatment and not as a method of spiritual enlightenment which uncovers past lives. However, on the other hand, many *do* believe in reincarnation, especially in the East, and they see Reiki, first and foremost, as a lofty spiritual method!

Among Reiki healers, there is a certain fear of the images which appear during a treatment. We wish to improve the spiritual and emotional health of the patient, and therefore our approach must be a positive one – emphasizing the good within him. However, during the Reiki treatment, the curtains veiling past lives are lifted, and what we see is not always positive, and certainly not always flattering to the patient. I often see spine-chilling images. In one case, I saw a bloody scenario worse than any scene in the most violent of movies. It seemed that the patient, a pleasant man (so I thought!), had been a soldier in an unidentified eastern empire in his last life, mainly occupied with burning and destroying entire towns.

(During lengthy treatments, it turned out that this man beat and abused his wife and children, probably as a result of the negative *karma* of which he had not rid himself. Almost a year of treatments was required to deal with this difficult condition.) In other cases, I uncover situations from past lives which have a negative influence on people in their present life. For example, a common image is of rape or sexual abuse, which occurred in earlier lifetimes, and in all instances, the victims, both men and women, suffered severe sexual problems in their present lifetime.

Reiki experts, and especially great masters, are able to accompany a patient on a journey into the unconscious to past lives, their advantage being that they can see clearly what the patient can only view in a hazy manner. My esteemed teacher, Master Naharo, would describe my former lifetimes, and his descriptions seemed familiar. I felt as if everything he described already existed within me. On one occasion, I nodded my head following one description or another, indicating that it seemed familiar to me. The difference being, of course, that the Master saw the entire picture with clarity and in detail, while I just viewed parts of the image with hazy vision.

Today, I know for sure that the relationship between Reiki and reincarnation is a connection of "removing obstacles"; in other words, Reiki removes the obstacles which prevent cosmic energy from flowing and from joining personal energy. It also removes obstacles which prevent an individual from seeing his former lives. In general, the more balanced the relationship between a person's body-mind-soul, the *less* he needs Reiki and the better he sees his previous incarnations. The opposite is also true: The *less* balanced a person is in body-mind-soul because of numerous energy blockages, the *more* he requires Reiki, as he is not able to see his former lives clearly.

When a Reiki treatment is performed, its main aim being to build bridges to former lives, the patient must lie on his stomach. The Reiki expert stands on the patient's right side, passing his palms along his spine, over his head (parallel to the forehead, or third-eye chakra, but not parallel to the head or crown chakra, which is higher), and to the middle of the back (parallel to the heart chakra). In other words, the treatment focuses on the third-eye, the throat and heart chakras, energy centers which are "in charge" of reincarnation.

The Reiki expert must focus his mind and actively seek the key which will enable him to penetrate the secrets of former lives. This is done with the help of meditative focusing. Each expert has his own symbols and word sequences which help him concentrate during treatment.

Does Reiki Inspire Love?

It started with a story that sounded like a romantic novel and ended with a deep comprehension of the Reiki of Love. It began with a married couple who exemplified everything a marriage or shared life should not be – quarrels, separations, malicious gossip, long periods without sexual relations, as a way to punish each other, and even mutual complaints to the police... and ended in a way that might do any love story with a happy ending proud!

Ronnie, the wife, was what one might call a "crystal freak", while Chris, her husband, was the biggest square I have ever encountered. When they got married, both were very mature. They had comfortable careers (Chris was an expert in accounting for sports teams and Ronnie an accomplished chemist with impressive work in the area of the research of industrial enzymes), and everyone was sure that their marriage would be a success story.

Over a period of three years, I watched their marriage fall apart right in front of my eyes. Ronnie, a smiling energetic woman, became angry, fatigued and depressed, and Chris found himself involved in numerous rows and arguments. It was terrible.

I do not remember why I suggested that Ronnie try Reiki treatments, as I usually refrain from treating close friends. However, I suggested it and she agreed. When she came for her first treatment, I felt the heavy burden which she was carrying on her slender shoulders. It was a difficult experience that I would not care to repeat.

But the treatment was effective. Ronnie began to smile again, her eyes shone and her step was light. In a pub where he had been drinking too much, I spontaneously offered Chris, her husband, a similar treatment. At first, he was so enraged that he almost hit me in the face. After a while, he agreed.

So I spent time with each of them over a period of several weeks. Ronnie came on Mondays and Wednesdays, and Chris on Tuesdays and Thursdays. The results were visible and rapid. However, I began to feel the weight of the burden that each of them had unburdened from themselves.

I suggested that they both come to the class in which I taught beginners the principles of Reiki.

They each arrived separately... but left the lesson with their arms around each other! And in my opinion, I think this is the essence of the story.

Following this case, I began to notice a phenomenon which at the time astounded me. Among couples who came to Reiki classes *together*, warm and loving relationships developed. One heart appeared to beat in two bodies. During the lesson, even when they sat far apart, they constantly exchanged smiles and glances.

I know that an individual who is somewhat familiar with Reiki, would make light of my amazement – since it is known that Reiki may be transmitted from a distance, and what is more natural than a gift of the Reiki of love, sent frequently from one partner to the other? What is so special about those smiles and glances?

The answer is simple. When a person concentrates, thinks about his beloved and sends her/him a gift of Reiki, it is done *consciously*. This is different from a couple sitting in a Reiki lesson whose good connection is created almost *without intention.*

An apprentice Reiki instructor from the east coast of the United States once claimed that couples in love are couples who "descended into the world together," that is, they are soulmates.

What better method is there to attract such souls to one another and open their avenues of communication than Reiki, which, amongst other things, opens communication channels to the pool of cosmic experience (which includes these two soulmates). However, I believe that the phenomenon is much broader. Reiki "opens" the individual, allows him to receive the feelings of love from his partner, and at the same time, to send his fullest love to her. Even when only one of the partners is studying or involved in Reiki, there is a positive effect on both of them: naturally, even greater when they are *both* immersed in Reiki.

With your permission, I will digress a little. The city of Poona in India is known as a center for gurus, among them many well-known Reiki Masters. Poona is also known as a center of "free love", and many imagine it is a center for sexual promiscuity and licentiousness. So it appears mainly to Westerners who come to Poona. (The locals, by nature, are much more conservative and reserved in their behavior.) When I first arrived in Poona, I was surprised to see many couples walking arm in arm, smiling at each another, with shining eyes and flushed cheeks. It seemed as if everyone was in love – no misery, no loneliness... It took me a number of years to understand that this was the result of the high concentration of Reiki experts and students; that the cause was Reiki and the result, love!

I do not wish to delude anyone. A couple who are not suited will not be helped by Reiki. At best, the treatment will open their eyes and help them to end their painful relationship. Reiki cannot repair a marriage or relationship between incompatible individuals. Reiki gives the couple an active, developing energy which allows them to be directed to a joint channel – *if they are suited* – or to a complete separation, if they are not.

It is important to emphasize that there is no connection between the Reiki of Love and the Reiki of Sex. By sex, I mean the ability to experience full and enjoyable sexual relations. Physically, for problems such as impotence, a lack of ability to experience orgasm (frigidity), vaginismus, premature ejaculation, painful intercourse, allergies related to sex (such as an allergy to semen), and so on, Reiki is one of the most effective methods of treatment (and maybe in this manner increases love). However, Reiki specialists differentiate completely between love and sex.

Moreover, out of ten Reiki students or patients, at least three will indicate that some sort of sexual problem induced them to try this method. Only one out of 20 will say that they turned to Reiki due to a lack of love or an obstacle obstructing their love.

The simple fact is that problems of love are treated primarily through the heart chakra, and secondarily through the throat chakra and the solar plexus chakra, while sexual problems are treated through the three lower chakras – the base chakra, the sex chakra and the solar plexus chakra. There is very little overlap.

The Reiki of Love is *always* performed in a standing position, with the healer facing the patient. His hands move from the sides inwards, as if wrapping the patient in the Reiki of Love.

The Reiki of Sex is done with the patient laying on his left side, in a fetal position, with the healer standing behind him, pushing the energy from the direction of the base chakra to the direction of the solar plexus chakra.

Afterword:
What *is* Reiki?

Now that you have read this book, you are probably feeling inspired and keen to try out this marvelous-sounding technique. You may still, however, be wondering what Reiki actually *is* - at a more profound level. In this afterword, we will try and elaborate on the subject and clarify some of the points that may still be in question.

Since ancient times, it has been commonly known that an invisible stream of energy flows through all living organisms. Despite modern-day skepticism and insistence upon empirical proof, recent medical and scientific research has verified the existence of this energy, and its role in the physical/emotional/spiritual healing process has been validated and acknowledged.

There are many healing processes that are based on the harnessing of this invisible energy. Most of them require years of study of philosophies, texts, doctrines, techniques, and so on, which often demand a high intellectual level, as well as a considerable amount of time.

The beauty of Reiki lies in its simplicity, in its accessibility to *everyone*. Our level of education or IQ is immaterial. The only thing that *is* significant here is our genuine desire to open ourselves to the energy that can heal our body and soul, and our willingness to take responsibility for our own well-being. We can achieve a level of spiritual transformation even if we do not meditate on a regular basis. Reiki initiation, that is, training or attunement, can be accomplished during a two-day course. If we are suitably receptive to the concept that underlies Reiki, we will be able to give ourselves and others beneficial, healing treatments by the end of that brief initiation process.

Reiki helps the body to release stress and tension by creating a state of profound relaxation which promotes healing and health, and a state of wholeness and balance.

In addition to the physical structure of the body, there is also a subtle energy system through which life force energy flows. This system consists of energy bodies which surround the physical body and help us process thoughts and emotions. The energy bodies have chakras, or energy centers, that regulate the flow of life force through the physical, mental, emotional and spiritual bodies. The life force energy nourishes us and balances our body's functions and systems.

Reiki has been defined as *spiritually guided life force energy* which is present everywhere. The Reiki system is a technique of transmitting energy into the human energy system via the hands. Reiki cleanses the body (that is, the physical and mental body) of toxins, and restores energy balance and vitality by relieving the harmful effects of stress. It opens blocked chakras and meridians, clears the energy bodies, and leaves us relaxed and at peace, with a feeling of profound mental purification.

Reiki treatment is warm, gentle, enveloping, comforting and nurturing; it creates a feeling of spontaneous joy and glowing radiance. Reiki treats the *whole* person: body, mind, emotions and spirit. It is easy to learn; we all can tap into the infinite pool of life force energy, improve our health and enhance our quality of life either by learning the technique and practicing it or by undergoing a treatment by a Reiki practitioner.

Reiki is simple and safe; there are no risks attached to it. Not only is it absolutely harmless, but it is beneficial to all of us. It can never be misused because it is always healing. It heals by flowing through the afflicted parts of the energy field and charging them with positive energy. It raises the level of the vibrations of the energy field in and around the physical body where there are negative thoughts and feelings, breaks these harmful factors up and dispels them. Reiki clears, straightens and heals energy pathways so that life force energy can flow naturally and unimpeded once again.

Reiki can also work in our unconscious realm and eliminate negative thoughts and feelings by breaking them up and washing them away. Thus it enables the normal healthy life force energy flow to resume and restore health.

However, these unconscious negative thoughts and feelings are problematic, because we ourselves are often unaware of their existence and are therefore unable to direct ourselves to change or get rid of them.

The word *Reiki*, as we already know, consists of two Japanese words, *Rei* and *Ki*. While the meaning of *Ki* is fairly straightforward and agreed upon, the meaning of *Rei* is far more complex. Its interpretations range from a rather simplistic meaning - *universal* - to far-reaching metaphysical concepts.

Rei: This is the infinite Higher Intelligence which guides the creation and functioning of the universe and is the source of guidance in our lives. It is the wisdom of God, or the High Power, or God-consciousness; it is supernatural knowledge and spiritual consciousness. It understands and knows each person completely, as it is omniscient and omnipresent. *Rei* knows the cause of all problems and difficulties, and how to heal them.

Ki: This is life force energy that animates everything, that is, gives life. *Ki* is a vital life force which flows through us via the chakras and meridians. It is also found around us, in the aura that surrounds every one of us. It is necessary for life force energy to flow freely in and around the body in order to maintain health. The source of *Ki* is in the air, food, sunshine and sleep. *Ki* can be increased by breathing exercises and meditation. If there is a high level of *Ki*, we are strong, confident, enjoy life and are capable of facing challenges. A low level of *Ki* means a low life force, diminished body and mind functioning, and consequently vulnerability to disease. *Ki* is a source of health in and around a person, rather than just the functioning and condition of physical organs and tissues. *Ki* animates and nourishes the organs, cells and tissues, and is responsible for enhancing vital functions. It is the primary energy of emotions, thoughts and spiritual life. When *Ki* leaves the physical body, the body dies.

Ki responds to our thoughts and emotions. The strength of its flow depends on the quality of our thoughts and feelings. Stress resulting from conflicting and negative thoughts and feelings can lead to a blockage in the energy system. These negative factors can be manifestations of fear, anger, anxiety, worry or doubt, and they are capable of blocking the body's ability to safeguard and maintain itself. The disruption in the flow of *Ki* is the cause of malfunction and illness. The vast majority of illnesses result from the mind; this has been acknowledged even in the West. However, it must be stressed that the mind is not situated only in the brain, but in the whole body, in all the systems and in the aura. Therefore, negative thoughts and feelings are not just limited to the brain; when they occur, they are present all over the body and in the aura, and their influence will be felt. If negative feelings cause *Ki* disruptions in a particular part of the body, the organs or systems there will be affected, resulting in malfunction and disease. It is important to eliminate negative thoughts and feelings as quickly as possible.

It is the God-consciousness, or *Rei*, that guides the life force, or *Ki*, in the healing technique called *Reiki*, which guides itself with its own infinite wisdom. Reiki energy knows where it is needed and creates the healing conditions for the particular person. Reiki is not guided by the mind, and is therefore independent of the limits or experience of any particular healer. Because there is no need to guide Reiki, as there is in other healing energies, Reiki energy begins to flow without the necessity for entering an altered state (such as deep meditation).

Reiki is not a religion. It has no dogma and no set of mandatory beliefs. In fact, it works without beliefs, because they are not important. What *is* necessary to Reiki, however, is that we live life in harmony with the world; this will bring us well-being. It is therefore important to practice certain simple ethical ideals in order to promote peace and harmony. These are the five principles which you read about at the beginning of this book:

Do not be angry.

Do not worry.

Be grateful.

Live a life of honor.

Honor your parents, honor your teachers, honor your elders.

The purpose of these principles is to help us realize that healing the spirit by consciously deciding to improve ourselves is a necessary part of the Reiki healing experience. For a long-lasting effect, we must take responsibility for our own healing, as well as an active part in it. Reiki therefore requires a conscious and active commitment to improving ourselves in order for it to be a complete system.

The Reiki healer does not direct the healing or decide what to work on, and therefore there is no danger of his/her taking on the patient's karma. The healer's non-involvement enables God-consciousness to shine through unimpeded. In addition, the healer's energies are never depleted, because Reiki knows that both healer and patient require healing, so both receive treatment simultaneously.

Giving a treatment, therefore, increases energy, love and well-being for both the healer and the patient.

Reiki is different from other healing methods because its energy can only be channeled by someone who has received initiation from a Reiki Master. Non-Reiki practitioners who have undergone Reiki initiation have reported an immense increase in the strength of their healing energies after their initiation; their energies are more powerful and of a much higher frequency.

In conclusion, it seems that most, if not all, people would benefit from Reiki treatments. Feeling better about ourselves and about our surroundings is probably the first step toward making our planet a more peaceful and harmonious place to live. Our attitude toward our fellow man would be one of increased tolerance and love, and the issues of nature and its preservation would be high on the list of priorities. Reiki is capable of creating an atmosphere of respect toward our surroundings, both in human and in natural terms.